Hotel Monteleone

More than a landmark, the heart of New Orleans since 1886

Text by Jenny Adams, Research by William D. Reeves
Introduction by Richard Ford

THE
DONNING COMPANY
PUBLISHERS

Copyright © 2011 by Hotel Monteleone

All rights reserved, including the right to reproduce this work in any form whatsoever without permission in writing from the publisher, except for brief passages in connection with a review. For information, please write:

The Donning Company Publishers
184 Business Park Drive, Suite 206
Virginia Beach, VA 23462

Steve Mull, General Manager
Barbara Buchanan, Office Manager
Pamela Koch, Senior Editor
Cindy Smith, Project Research Coordinator
Tonya Hannink, Marketing Specialist
Pamela Engelhard, Marketing Advisor

Neil Hendricks, Project Director

Book Design: Phillip Collier Designs, New Orleans, LA

Library of Congress Cataloging-in-Publication Data

Adams, Jenny, 1980-
  Hotel Monteleone : more than a landmark, the heart of New Orleans since 1886 / text by Jenny Adams ; research by William D. Reeves.
       p. cm.
  ISBN 978-1-57864-654-8 (hard cover : alk. paper)
 1. Hotel Monteleone–History. 2. Hospitality industry–Louisiana–New Orleans–History. 3. New Orleans–History. I. Reeves, William D. (William Dale), 1941- II. Title.
  TX941.H685A33 2010
  647.94763'35–dc22
                        2010040625

Printed in the United States of America at Walsworth Publishing Company

Early twentieth century photograph of the Hotel Monteleone made from the roof of the Maison Blanche building looking toward the Mississippi River.

TABLE OF CONTENTS

Introduction
by Richard Ford 7

Chapter 1
Early History 10

Chapter 2
Growth of the Hotel. 30

Chapter 3
Food and Entertainment 54

Chapter 4
Prose, Plots, and Bon Vivants 70

y most enduring memory of the Monteleone—and my most endearing—must've originated about 1950. I was six. It was a typical shoe-leather-melting summer day in New Orleans. My mother, to while away the steamy hours and divert her only son, had been taking us back and forth across on the Algiers Ferry for most of an afternoon, letting me stand up in the bow, breathing in the hot, complex, brackishness of the river, watching the city's modest skyline move away, then draw close again, move away, come near, move away. Pralines are a central feature of this memory. They were on sale at the ferry dock, packaged in small, waxy sleeves, and sold for a dime.

At five sharp, however, we quit our journeying and walked hand in hand up Canal Street, the short stroll to Royal and down the shadowy block and a half to the Monteleone, which was my father's "headquarters" when he worked his south Louisiana accounts—Schwegmann's and Delchamps in town, and all the small wholesale grocer concerns down through Houma and over to Lake Charles, up to Villeplatte and Alec, and back again. He sold laundry starch. Faultless. It was a name that meant something then. He'd be waiting for us in the hotel.

When we arrived, we found him seated on a stool in the Carousel Bar, just to the right, inside the hotel entrance where it still is today, its windows facing onto Royal to let the patrons watch the world go by outside from within, where it's cool. My mother and I sat down beside my father at the circular bar. They were happy to see each other after a long hot day apart. Our family was only the three of us. But my father had a look of consternation on his long Irish lip, and his brow was furrowed, a familiar expression that meant things weren't going well. "Carrol, what's the matter?" my mother said. "You look worried."

"I don't know." My father shook his head as if to exhibit confusion. "I've just had one drink. But I guess it made me drunk. Because when I came in here twenty minutes ago, I sat down at this bar and I could've sworn I was facing the door—so I'd see you. But now I'm facing the window. I don't know what's happening to me."

My mother told this story with relish all her life. I suppose I'll tell it all of mine. To her it proved what a sweetly guileless man my father was, a country boy, unsophisticated in the ways of big cities, trusting to how things should be, not so sure about a world where the elegant bar in a swell hotel could imperceptibly make a complete revolution every fifteen minutes, taking its unsuspecting tipplers along for the ride; a ride they might not—if they were

my father—even notice they were taking. Carousel. The name might've suggested something, but didn't. That guilelessness was partly why she loved him all her life. I always have a drink there when I'm around, think sweetly of the two of them all those years ago in the Monteleone.

I guess one has to say—in view of memories like mine—that the best thing today about the stately old Monteleone (now 125 years young) is that it's still here, its latch-string still on the outside, its brassy doors still swinging open to drummers like my father, to vacationers down from Des Moines, newlyweds overnighting for a slice of heaven, legislators cutting midnight deals, executives with their secretaries in tow, Arab sheiks, movie types, goateed jazz-men, gigolos and gigolettes, the odd writer needing refuge to polish his story in a room that sees the river. If you would read closely, at the conclusion of Eudora Welty's magnificent New Orleans story "No Place for You, My Love," you'd see (at least I see) the heroine of this sumptuous, passion-streaked story, alighting from her lover's convertible and disappearing through the revolving doors of a hotel. It's this hotel. It could scarcely be any other.

So, yes—or no. The Monteleone's still here after 125 years, cradling my memories and a million others'. It hasn't fallen to the greed and stingy imagination of the entrepreneurial spirit and its dumb wrecking ball, which only seems to clear a way for hotels of ersatz grandeur and un-nuanced chrome and glass predictability that calls itself hospitality. Me—the inveterate stayer in a thousand hotel rooms in my life—I'm on the run from those spiritless places. And where I run to is here.

Oh, there used to be hotels like this one—or at least close: old, family-owned, family-run accommodations all across the south, all across America. The Muehlebach in K.C. The Peabody in Memphis. The Marion in Little Rock. The Edwards in Jackson. The Bentley in Alexandria. The Drake in Chicago. A few persist today, it's true: genuine hotels—not "venues," not "properties" with corporate ice in their veins and precisely planned obsolescence; but honest-to-God *establishments*, where arriving and checking in was a ceremonious event all its own, with public-private formalities and rituals and assumptions and a cast of memorable employee-characters that all joined in declaring to the weary traveler or the grinning, winking old pol or the young bride and groom: "You're not at home now. This is special. You're our guest, not just a customer. We offer comfort and privacy for whatever you require comfort and privacy *for*. But we'd also like you to feel you belong here, at least for a while."

Obviously I'm a romantic when it comes to these splendiferous old piles and their gilded trappings—chandeliers and chimes, goldfish ponds and red damask wall coverings, liveried this's and that's. I hope I won't live long enough to see them go extinct. Later in my boyhood I actually resided in one, and in my time I saw parade before me a thousand florid stories, characters, spectacles—a great Scheherazade of a place, featuring (it seemed) the world's moral miscellany passing every day: pathos, transgression, charity, humblings large and small, unsavoriness and kindness of every stamp. Much of it extremely funny. Not a bad beginning for a boy on his way to be a writer. And I've lived long enough to see even that old place of my boyhood torn down, imploded, and a gleaming new ziggurat rise from its rubble. The Excelsior, they called the new place. Quite glittering. And now it's gone, too, after only thirty years, replaced by something different—all my faithful memories left with no firm locus on which to fix themselves, just afloat, surviving in my dreams.

Which brings me quick to the end here—and you to the beginning.

Best of all worlds? Near the other end of life now, I'd like to live here (again, as it were), maybe just down the hall from where you are today; make permanent and caressing what's so fleeting and rare—the ceremony, the observance and protocol, the sense of affirmation that a place like the Monteleone confers. A certain kind of estimating, untrusting man *wants* to live out his winter years discreetly in a good hotel—where Al the bellman knows your name, where the bartender pours your drink before you even get there, where the sheets are crisp each night and the towels plentiful and fresh, your breakfast eggs are poached perfect each morning; and where, when you step out onto Royal Street to calculate the day, the doorman steps up with a grin and says, "Another beauty, Mr. Ford" (whether it is or it isn't). I could let time ease by that way, you bet I could—which is to say timelessly, barely noticed—the way it passes in a good story that you read again and again and again, always wanting more.

Richard Ford
1215 Burgundy Street
New Orleans, 2010

CHAPTER 1
Early History

he story of this hotel, from its physical proportions to its long-tenured employees, opens with the single man from whom she takes her name. Antonio Monteleone was born in 1855 in Contessa, Sicily, and as a young man in the 1880s, he moved to New Orleans with grand dreams and scant provisions. While history will forever remember him as pioneering one of America's most legendary hotel properties, this hotel is much more than one man's endeavor. It's an institution that evolved thanks to a city's people who were filled with both idealistic dreams and sordid transgressions. Like the city it calls home, the Hotel Monteleone is standing testament to the collective menagerie of characters that have walked through her doors. They have each left a mark—from bellmen employed for decades to managers who changed both policy and history to struggling writers quietly scratching the first lines of unforgettable literature in the lobby bar.

While without Antonio Monteleone this hotel surely would have never existed, there were myriad players throughout history, all crucial to making his vision reality. This story is a testimony to their efforts as well as to Mr. Monteleone's hard work, striking vision and countless triumphs. In everything that is the Hotel Monteleone—the fine service, the devotion to detail, the people who were both born to find a home here and those who have remained as unforgettable ghosts—125 years seems like a brief period of time to accomplish so much.

Antonio Monteleone is remembered as a great entrepreneur. However, his first endeavors lay farther south and were, literally and figuratively, less lofty than creating what is today the largest hotel in the French Quarter. Monteleone entered the business world in the French Quarter of New Orleans, or "the Vieux Carré," as a cobbler.

Reports note a Francis Monteleone as a shoemaker in the year 1879, and one year later, in 1880, there is a listing for a

They say that time heals all wounds, but in the case of New Orleans and the Italians trying to make a better life on American shores, it was a combination of time and very hard work.

Opposite page:
Antonio Monteleone (1855-1913).

Frank Monteleone in the business of "boots and shoes," at 80 Royal Street. It is likely that Frank Monteleone was Antonio's uncle. The young Antonio would come into his own standing officially three years later, when his name appeared in the City Directories in capital letters as a shoemaker working from the same address at 80 Royal Street. Capital letters in the directories were an indication of importance and fine standing in that day. From 1884 until 1889, Antonio worked at this address, now 241 Royal, the corner where the street connects to Bienville. During these years, he met and married Sophia Jahraus, the couple welcoming three sons and a daughter, Anthony V., Bernardo, Stella and Frank.

In those years, families like the Monteleones were becoming more and more common in the Quarter. Sicilians seeking a better life in this portion of the city were so familiar, in fact, the then poorer French Quarter was often referred to as "Little Sicily" or "Little Palermo." New Orleans in particular was drawing them like children to sunlight, Sicilians opting for the warmer, southern shore over the continental Italians, who were arriving most frequently by way of Ellis Island. By 1890 New Orleans reportedly counted 30,000 Italian Americans as residents. From 1891 to 1892, the number of Italians arriving in New Orleans totaled 5,644, and the majority of them were Sicilians.[1]

They had a great influence on the city's history. Italian American social clubs in the city date back prior to the Civil War, and the specifically Sicilian groups flourished in the years just following it.

Today, the world considers New Orleans one of America's most lauded culinary enclaves, thanks in part to the Sicilian influence on cuisine during the last decades of the nineteenth century. They began showcasing a gift for cooking and service through a variety of mom-and-pop operations—from bakeries to restaurants to hotels in the 1890s and beyond. One prominent example is the city's penchant for the Muffuletta sandwich. It was created at the Central Grocery on Decatur in 1906.[2]

Several of the cherished cultural nuances of New Orleans are traced back to the Italian Americans. Nick La Rocca, for example, was born to poor Sicilian American immigrants in the city in the spring of 1889. He rose during the early 1900s to be

By 1890 New Orleans reportedly counted 30,000 Italian Americans as residents.

considered one of the first creators of jazz. His 1917 composition "Tiger Rag" has been deemed one of the most important and influential jazz standards of the twentieth century, with 136 cover versions recorded by 1942 alone.

But it was not all breezy social gatherings and warm, hearty meals. During the late 1800s, the Italian immigrants in particular were suspect in the city, especially disliked by the Irish immigrants who had a stronger, more tenured presence. Discrimination, racism, stereotyping and suspicion against Sicilians was fueled and made legitimate by the Italian Mafia's presence in the city. The Mafia actually began in Sicily, with the word loosely translating as "manly." The immigrants who were previously tied to it in their homeland quickly set up operations in New Orleans. The city was the stage for the first major Mafia incident in America, on October 15, 1890, when Police Chief David Hennessey was murdered. More than one hundred Sicilian immigrants were arrested and jailed. Nine men were finally indicted for Hennessey's murder, and the subsequent acquittal led to claims of bribery and witness intimidation. A lynch mob attacked the pardoned, killing eleven of the nineteen defendants.[3]

The story made national news headlines, and reparations were paid to the families by the United States government.[4]

They say that time heals all wounds, but in the case of New Orleans, and the Italians trying to make a better life on American shores, it was a combination of time and very hard work. The reputable Italian immigrants fought to gain status in the city, and through grit and determination, the responsible efforts eventually paid off. However, New Orleans would not know her first Italian mayor until much later, in 1936 with the election of Robert Maestri.

Antonio Monteleone was certainly one of the most recognizable and most reputable Sicilians in the city in the late 1800s and early 1900s. Even as a cobbler, he quickly began to exercise his unique skills with machinery. Besides being particularly adept with moveable parts, he understood the benefits to a business of mass production with the help of machines. One month following his death in 1913, the August 6 *Daily Picayune* published an account of the man behind the hotel in his early years as a shoemaker.

It eulogized, "He saved his money carefully, and leaving his employer, opened a shoe store at St. Louis and Royal Streets,

In the late 1800s the French Quarter was sometimes referred to as "Little Sicily" because of the large influx of Italian immigrants.

in an old building since torn down to make way for the new Courthouse. He prospered and in a few years he moved a block further up, opening a larger store at Conti and Royal, opposite the old mortgage office. All the while Mr. Monteleone was figuring on machines, both as a means to speed and to perfection in making shoes, and when, by frugality he had amassed enough money he rented the building at Bienville and Royal Streets, bought a number of machines, and so started the first shoe factory in New Orleans."[5]

History would not paint Antonio as a struggling immigrant or as a simple cobbler. While his work establishing the city's first shoe factory would point to his promise, it would be hotels that would forever mark his influence in the Big Easy. Antonio was determined to rise in the city, amidst the grime of the French Quarter, beyond the prostitution and corruption, despite his beginnings as a foreigner in a constantly struggling environment.

Unlike his less-fortunate, olive-skinned countrymen who toiled alongside the African Americans on the docks or fell prey to the pressures to join with the Mafia, Antonio began saving money at every available opportunity and investing what he was able to amass in various real estate ventures.

According to the Conveyance Office Records in Orleans Parish, his first major purchase of land with a building was recorded on July 26, 1882. The acquisition was near Decatur between Frenchman and Elysian Fields in what known as the Marigny. He purchased it at auction for $900.[6] Bidding on property in this manner grew on Antonio, and he began swiftly acquiring, including another lot and building in the square bounded by Bienville, Customhouse, Dauphine and Burgundy. He paid $2,000 for a property in the 900 block of Bienville, followed by two lots on St. Peter that he and his wife Sophia bought jointly.[7]

In 1884, he bought his third property for $3,000, a twenty-five-foot stretch on St. Philip Street, between Chartres and Decatur. However, none of these were anywhere in proximity—in size or location—to what would become his legendary Hotel Monteleone.[8]

It was 1886 when he finally acquired a building close to the current hotel's site, a full block contained by Royal, Bienville, Conti, and Chartres. This corner lot that faced Bienville and

> *History would not paint Antonio as a struggling immigrant or as a simple cobbler. While his work establishing the city's first shoe factory would point to his promise, it would be hotels that would forever mark his influence in the Big Easy.*

Opposite page:
In the entrance to the building on the corner of Royal and Bienville–across from what is the present day hotel–you can still see the Monteleone crest in mosaic tile. Previously, the building housed one of Antonio Monteleone's many cobbler shops.

Royal had the address of 54 Royal. It became the family home, and Antonio moved his wife Sophia and children in, with the property remaining in his possession until his death in 1913. Their home would have been adjacent to the present hotel. The street numbers began changing during this time, and years later it was reassigned with the address of 241 Royal. The cost recorded for the big block was $10,100—a considerable purchase for the day.[9]

Antonio's first hotel was a three-story townhouse on the corner of Iberville and Royal Streets. By 1894 he would have been considered a serious hotel proprietor, evident in city directory statements that claim, while he was still listed as "shoe manfr. 200 and 241 Royal, r. same," he was also the owner of the building which housed the Hotel Victor, run by a proprietress, Mrs. Louise Bero. Antonio was selling shoes downstairs, while Mrs. Bero showed guests to their rooms above. Eventually, his shoe operation moved—but not far. He purchased the corner lot across from Royal and relocated his manufacturing business there.[10] In 1896, he expanded the townhouse on Iberville and Royal into a five-story operation, and as the decade came to a close, Antonio began to show great confidence in a man named James D. Kenney. With Kenney as his hotel manager, he took over the property entirely. The Hotel Victor fell in line with trend of the changing street numbers and changed its name to the Commercial Hotel. A stay in the Commercial Hotel would have run you $1 a day that year, with an additional cost tacked on if you wanted a bath.[11] It was one of the few properties that could afford—and found reason—to advertise in the *Daily Picayune*. Competing advertisers included the St. Charles Mansion, the Hotel Denechaud and the Hotel Grunewald.

If previous years might be painted by Antonio's relentless movement in New Orleans, acquiring buildings and land parcels the way a skilled chess player focuses on capturing pawns, with his signature on the Commercial, he became a man focused on a queen—a sole building and what it might grow to become. James D. Kenney was influential on Antonio Monteleone, backing him on his belief that expansion was necessary. The Commercial unfolded to incorporate first 208–210 Royal, followed by the purchase and addition of the Duncan Buildings along

> *Antonio's first hotel was a three-story townhouse on the corner of Iberville and Royal Streets. By 1894 he would have been considered a serious hotel proprietor.*

Opposite page:
The Hotel Victor would eventually become the Commercial Hotel, which then became the Hotel Monteleone. This photo shows Hotel Victor in the 1890s.

Exchange Alley. In the three subsequent connected lots tacked on to those, we find in present day the oldest section of the current Hotel Monteleone.

The hotel would finally come into being in 1909 under the name "Hotel Monteleone," with the distinction of being Antonio's third hotel.

If you were to stroll down the cobblestones during these last years of the nineteenth century and the first dawn of the twentieth, a few of the other buildings surrounding Antonio's growing empire included a massive, three-story mansion overlooking Royal, identified on the Sanborn map as a restaurant and gambling den. There was the Palais Royal at No. 36 Royal, which showcased free variety acts and doubled as a concert saloon. Numbers 38 and 40 on the street were second-hand furniture and auction houses, and moving on down to No. 42, you would have found another concert saloon named the Park Theater. You could have dropped off laundry in one half of the Chinese-run operation at No. 50 Royal or gotten your umbrella fixed in the storefront's other half.[12]

The French Quarter's personality changed drastically after the Civil War ended, and it continued evolving rapidly in the first decade of the twentieth century. Prior to the war, it was home to the hardworking lower classes, a mix of immigrants from all over Europe like the Monteleones and their Sicilian brothers; however, after the turn of the century, the area began to morph into a center of mischievous arts and wanton revelry.

In 1886, we know for certain that the Park Theater at 42 Royal debuted as the new Eden Theater, and although named presumably for Adam and Eve's biblical paradise, the spot flaunted sinful entertainment with a misleading tagline as "the only strictly legitimate Vaudeville theatre in the South." Owned by a man named Otto Schoenhausen and managed by F. Bastide, the Eden Theater's capacity was listed at 1,500 people, and it advertised a second floor with a Grand Café, salons, promenades and private parlors offering a "measurable secrecy from view."[13]

The club's grandeur and opulent areas of discretion were short lived, however. A fire in 1891 claimed the Eden entirely, at the same time destroying several buildings in the 200 block of Royal. Antonio's corner investment at 30 Royal was only kissed lightly by flames and suffered minor damage.[14]

The hotel would finally come into being in 1909 under the name "Hotel Monteleone," with the distinction of being Antonio's third hotel.

Opposite page:
A stay in the Commercial Hotel, shown here, would have cost you $1 per day. The Commercial would eventually become the Hotel Monteleone in the year 1909.

Otto Schoenhausen would make headlines for another property during these years—fighting for capitalism no matter the consequences on fine living and propriety. The families residing in the area filed a lawsuit against him. They claimed his Union Bank Saloon and Restaurant—named that because the spot was, in fact, previously the Union Bank—was morally reprehensible and bringing the neighborhood to its knees. Looking back now, it's a bit comical that the property housing the Union Bank Saloon and Restaurant was actually owned by the Tommy Lafon Asylum for Boys.[15]

Schoenhausen's courtroom argument speaks to the state of the French Quarter during this time, with his defense claiming that the area was already so tawdry and wicked, his saloon couldn't possibly affect it one way or the other. His lawyers plied jurors with an opening statement and the following description of this particular portion of the Vieux Carré.

"In fact, this locality is dedicated to avocations usually regarded as disreputable and illegitimate. It belongs to the same class of amusements as the concert halls, which are to be seen all over the continent of Europe, upon the most fashionable streets of Paris and other metropolitan cities. The exhibitions and performances given there are not near as indecent as those of the 'Moulin Rouge,' or even in the 'Jardin de Paris,' situated on the Champs-Elysees, the grandest boulevard on the face of the earth."[16]

As a neighboring business owner, Antonio Monteleone was asked to take the stand by the attorney for the plaintiffs, a Mr. Lazarus.[17] At this time, Antonio was still operating his shoe factory downstairs at the Hotel Victor on the corner of Iberville and Royal, with Mrs. Louise Bero overseeing the hotel rooms above. In the trial transcripts, Antonio calls Schoenhausen's operation the worst "place I ever see in the civilization of people." He continued that he and his wife occasionally "jump from the bed and hear the noise that the women make, and sometimes a fellow hit them."

Lazarus asked Monteleone if he was happy with his location, to which he replied: "I am sorry I built it since Schoenhausen is there now."

Advertisements began to run as early as January 1898, touting the brand new look and design of Monteleone's Commercial

This photo shows businesses down Exchange Alley at the turn of the twentieth century.

Hotel. Rooms, priced at a dollar, were lower than the competitors like the Grunewald and Royal Hotel, and Antonio also helped out his neighboring restaurateur Jules Alciatore, proprietor of Antoine's restaurant, by promoting the Commercial's proximity to the Vieux Carré's best French eateries. Other fine points like front and south exposure for the rooms, steam heat, electric elevators and electric lights were also mentioned.[18]

In 1902, Antonio purchased a parcel on the west side of Exchange Alley called the Duncan Building from L. Bonquois for a price of $19,000 and doubled the Commercial's square-foot land allotment. He proudly announced that he and Kenney would begin demolition in the summer to add one hundred rooms with private baths. The plan for private bathrooms was a lavish extravagance for any hotel in America, and the men became pioneers in the area of guest comforts away from home. For Monteleone and Kenney, the declaration and decision was a symbol of pride and faith they felt in a burgeoning New Orleans.[19]

Although there is no source identified, a newspaper clipping also notes some $200,000 was spent on redecorating and remodeling the Commercial, and a restaurant inside that faced the corner of Royal and Iberville. Monteleone's money funded touches like genuine marble pillars inside the oyster house, and he purchased grand chandeliers for the office of the hotel, the restaurant and café.

"Specially cast of brass...[they] are ponderous yet handsome affairs weighting 300 pounds each," the article states. The remodel article also discussed twelve new bathrooms and sparkling new suites on the second floor.

The following year, the Columbia Brewery purchased the buildings on Iberville across Exchange Alley behind Monteleone's Commercial Hotel, and we know at this point, from shoes to brews, that Monteleone was a major investor in the brewery. The hotel and beer men of the day were a joined sort. By 1908 the building housed the Schutten Hotel, with a large beer parlor on the ground floor.[20]

In addition to guests lounging in private bubble baths, standing amongst the lobby's marble columns or savoring oysters fresh from the gulf, Monteleone's hotel improvements in these days also included safety measures that would prevent damage from one

Advertisements began to run as early as January 1898, touting the brand new look and design of Monteleone's Commercial Hotel. Rooms, priced at a dollar, were lower than the competitors like the Grunewald and Royal Hotel.

of the most feared wraths of Mother Nature. It was not hurricanes, but fire. Fire was a considerable stress factor for business owners, and in the French Quarter's close quarters, once started, flames could mercilessly take down building after building in a matter of hours. Antonio had already had personal brushes with fire and would have surely considered his competitor's more disastrous misfortune when the famous St. Charles Hotel burned to the ground, taking four lives in the process.

To secure both his guests' lives and his own fortune, Monteleone began fireproofing his properties, and from 1900 to 1905, he stayed busy acquiring four separate thirty-three-foot lots. These would make up the nexus of his new grand vision and what we enjoy today as the Hotel Monteleone. New Orleans, like the rest of America, was in an era of opulence prior to the coming of the First World War. Celebratory toasts rang out nightly in bars around the French Quarter, and long, lavish dinners carried the weight of promising business deals and handshakes that would lead to lasting testaments in architecture and ambiance for the newly swelling tourism industry.

The newspaperman John S. Kendall surveyed the hotel scene of the first two decades of this century in about 1920, highlighting the progress of the hotel men.

He wrote:

> In addition to the St. Charles, New Orleans possesses at the present time a number of excellent hotels, of which the most prominent are the Hotel Grunewald, the Hotel de Soto, the Monteleone, the Lafayette, and the Planters'. The Hotel Grunewald was established on Baronne Street, near Canal, in 1893. The present magnificent structure, extending back through the square to University Place, dates from 1908. The DeSoto was opened in the spring of 1906. It is a magnificent building covering an entire square on Baronne and Poydras streets. The Monteleone was established in 1901, on Royal Street, one block below Canal Street. The Lafayette occupies a commanding location overlooking Lafayette Square. It was opened to the public in October, 1916. The Planters' Hotel,

To secure both his guests' lives and his own fortune, Monteleone began fireproofing his properties, and from 1900 to 1905, he stayed busy acquiring four separate thirty-three-foot lots. These would make up the nexus of his new grand vision and what we enjoy today as the Hotel Monteleone.

Opposite page:
Vintage map showing the French Quarter's layout and the Mississippi River.

formerly known as the Hotel Bruno, is situated on Dauphine Street, corner of Iberville. It was opened in 1906, and the building was renovated and refurnished in 1919.[21]

A contractor named George Glover was hired to build Antonio's vision, and he was chosen based on his reputation as the man who gave the city the important Beaux-Arts buildings, like the Whitney Bank, Canal Bank (NBC building), the D. H. Holmes building. In 1911, the local architectural journal *Architectural Art and Its Allies* wrote, "The Monteleone Hotel, from ground to dome, with its marvelously picturesque Lobby, is also a magnificent specimen of the work of Mr. Glover."[22]

For the architects, Monteleone chose the firm of Toledano & Wogan, who, according to the June 1907 *Times Picayune*, labeled the style "French Renaissance."

The first drawings illuminated an entrance set at thirty-two feet wide by forty-four feet long, comprised of a pressed brick and terra cotta, ornamental white façade. The ground floor was built for the lobby, but also included a ladies' parlor, café and dining room, a writing room, lavatory, barbershop, telegraph office, phone booths, cloak room, kitchen, storage and baggage handling room. Adorned in a Louis XIV style, mosaic floors would support marble columns and wainscoting ten feet high. A grand staircase was drawn in, spanning fourteen feet, leading to the second floor, but the hotel would offer two passenger elevators beside the entrance to the ladies' parlor, as well. The café promised carved oak with the relief of Bacchus, the god of wine, and vines reliefs wrapping the column tops. The palm court, done in an Italian Renaissance style, would seat 250 and adjoin the café.

The architects also designed 220 guest rooms, 160 of which with attached baths, and all with electric lighting, a telephone and mail chutes. There was meeting space and banquet facilities for two hundred on the eleventh floor, and a second ladies' parlor was available on the second floor opposite the elevators. On April 8, 1908, the City Engineer issued the construction permit for work to begin.

Mr. and Mrs. W. J. Kelly of St. Louis checked into the new hotel on November 26, 1908. They were counted as the first guests in the registry, and Mr. and Mrs. M. Dees of Biloxi were the first

For the architects, Monteleone chose the firm of Toledano & Wogan, who, according to the June 1907 *Times Picayune*, labeled the style "French Renaissance." These first drawings illuminated an entrance set at thirty-two feet wide by forty-four feet long, comprised of a pressed brick and terra cotta, ornamental white façade.

Opposite page:
Early 1900s postcard of Hotel Monteleone. Mr. and Mrs. W. J. Kelly of St. Louis were the first guests ever recorded on the hotel registry in 1909.

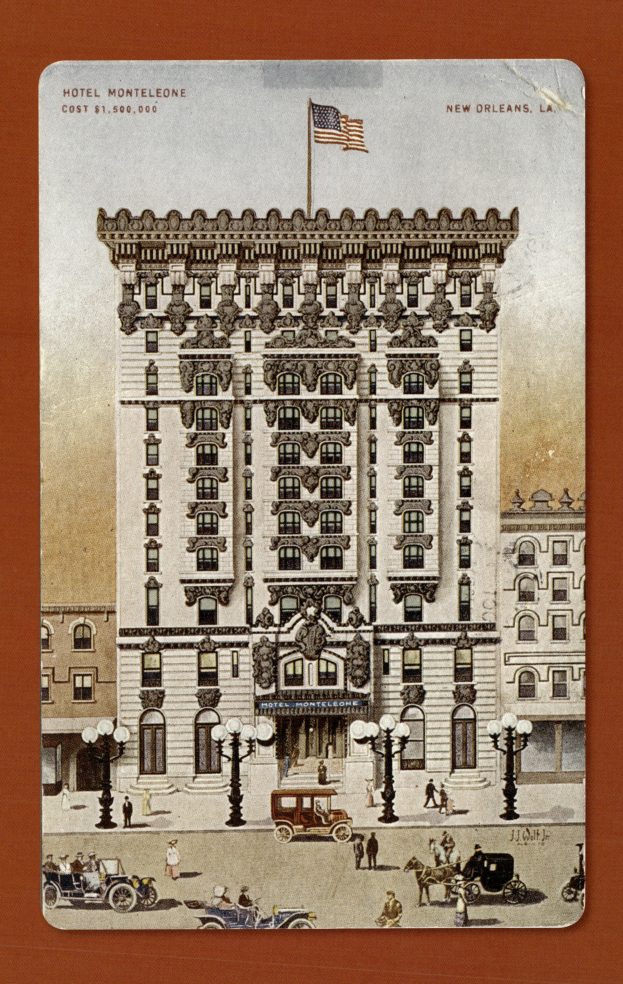

newlyweds to arrive for a honeymoon.[23] Inside the restaurant, the orchestra played some nights until 1 a.m., and in the year 1910, the *Daily Picayune* listed its members as Rose Montague on piano, Max Fink on violin, Luis Mejia playing the cello with Alphonse Majia on flute, and Sal Hernandez on clarinet.[24]

It wasn't all roses, flutes of champagne and dancing the darkness away during these years, however. Antonio Monteleone and other wealthy businessmen were continually harassed by the Mafia, and occasionally threatened with violence unless ransom demands were met. When asked his thoughts, the Sicilian-born Monteleone responded that he was not much bothered by the letters he received from the Mafia, and that it would be, "more difficult possibly for others, who have not heretofore have the experience."[25]

While he didn't have much to say to the Mafia in response to their demands, Antonio Monteleone had a great deal to say on behalf of workers who wished to organize. He was a proponent and champion of the union laborers, and he agreed to only use union members of the Boot and Shoe Workers Union in his manufacturing business when American Federation of Labor sent organizer Howard H. Caldwell down to New Orleans in 1901 to assemble workers.[26] After this point, the hotel even became a headquarters for union workers, and when the railway clerks for the Queen and Crescent Railroad went on strike in 1910, it was Antonio Monteleone who was able to negotiate a "quiet agreement" thanks to his standing in the community. The strike vote tallies were even stored in the hotel safe, but after the results

The hotel began producing its own line of chicory coffee available for guests in 1911, advertising the grandeur of the building and the rooms on the other side of the label.

were in and the strike was settled, they were taken outside secretly and burned.[27]

He was a respected man with a respected hotel, and though always a champion for the little guy, he mixed and mingled with the elite classes as well in the dawn of the 1900s, participating in Carnival yearly as one of the peers of Rex's court.[28]

He was also fond of European travel, and it was on a trip to Germany, while inside a German spa known as Bad Nauhelm, that Antonio Monteleone passed away at fifty-eight years old.[29] The *Daily Picayune* announced his death on July 21, 1913, and ran a lengthy article. One small excerpt read:

"Pioneer shoe manufacturer, hotel proprietor, banker, promoter and man of affairs generally, Mr. Monteleone held a conspicuous place in the public life of New Orleans and everybody knew him, either personally or by reputation. His rise to financial greatness is a story of ingenious struggle, tireless energy and the close application of natural talents to a high purpose."[30]

The newspaper's lead article went on to highlight the exact moment when the hotel staff was alerted in intense and poignant detail.

> John Rettenmeier, who was in charge of the New Monteleone Hotel while both Kenney and Monteleone were traveling, sat in his office yesterday morning arranging the details for the day's work, and looking over the terms of the $10,000 contract for the entire repainting of the interior of the hotel, let by Mr. Monteleone, just before his departure for Europe when a blue-coated Western Union messenger boy entered.
>
> Mr. Rettenbeier opened the telegram, and when his eyes scanned the second line he started up with surprise, the paper fluttering from his fingers and turning in circles on the floor under his desk in the teeth of the breeze from the electric fan. The line had read told the crushing story, "Mr. Monteleone died in Germany." Mr. Rettenmeir, reaching for the paper called loudly for one of the clerks...

...always a champion for the little guy, he mixed and mingled with the elite classes as well...

Guests to the hotel will find this oil portrait of Antonio Monteleone hanging in the lobby today.

Monteleone Gate

James D. Kenney, now married to Antonio's only daughter Stella Monteleone, was named as testamentary executor.

One of Antonio Monteleone's most considerable charitable contributions was erected in the year after his death and stands today. He donated the marble gates leading into City Park in 1912 to mark the same year the art museum began operation. The park's entrance in those years was on Lelong Street rather than Alexander where it stands currently. As the Park Commissioner, Antonio Monteleone donated the giant pylons that bear his name

between Beauregard Circle and Lelong Avenue. The construction began directly after he departed for Europe. According to Board President Paul Capdeville's report the following year, Monteleone "gave instructions to his architects to build a gate at the Esplanade entrance before leaving for Europe. Mr. Monteleone died while in Europe, but his heirs erected the marble gate."[31]

Money was also donated by his living heirs two years later to wire the twenty-five-foot pylons with eight bronze electric lamps.

HOTEL MONTELEONE
NEW ORLEANS

ABSOLUTELY FIRE-PROOF

"IN THE HEART OF THE CITY"

ROOMS:
WITHOUT BATH - 1.00 DAY and UP
WITH PRIVATE BATH ATTACHED - 2.00 DAY and UP

EUROPEAN PLAN
J. D. KENNEY, M..

CHAPTER 2
Growth of the Hotel

s the rooms and finer touches on the Hotel Monteleone evolved in the first decades of the twentieth century, James D. Kenney's involvement with the hotel grew in a personal nature as well. Married to Stella Monteleone, Kenney was, at the time of Antonio's death in 1913, not only his most trusted business confidant but also his son-in-law. Because Antonio's sons, Antonio Jr., William and Frank, were too young for such complicated matters at the time of his passing, the management of the hotel was left completely in Kenney's capable hands, and he was named the executor of Monteleone's estate and the managing director of business affairs throughout the 1920s.

Sadly, death would visit the Monteleone family three times in this decade, with the passing of Sophie Jahrens and sons Antonio Jr. and William. As he grew older, Frank Monteleone took over many of Kenney's responsibilities for the property.

While the family personally suffered loss, the hotel's growth was a counterbalance during these years. The price for a night in its lavish comforts was still set at $1, and by 1926 advertisements listed ceiling fans and radios in every single room.[32]

The lots at 222-224 and 226 Royal Street were purchased in 1916 and 1918 for the prices of $23,000 and $14,000 under Kenney's watchful eye, and they were scenes for further growth for the property. In 1926 Kenney signed the papers on the purchase of 232 Royal, beginning the third major addition to the hotel.[33]

Fifteen floors and a staggering two hundred rooms were added onto the wing across Royal Street. What is now the Queen Anne Ballroom was also erected in this third addition. It was known as the "Annex" then, and today it comprises the Bienville portion of the current hotel.

The price for a night in its lavish comforts was still set at $1, and by 1926 advertisements listed ceiling fans and radios in every single room.

Overleaf:
The Hotel Monteleone lobby as it looked in 1911.

Frank Monteleone.

In October of 1929, the stock market crash devastated the country and the rest of the industrialized nations of the western world. The Hotel Monteleone was the only hotel in New Orleans to remain open. Not only did the staff serve guests that day, but the hotel even gave guests money so that they could get home.

James D. Kenney moved to the position of managing director in the late twenties, and A. F. "Tony" Spatafora took over the position from 1936 until 1967. From an unidentified clipping, we glean a bit of information on the perks of the hotel in 1931.

"Our new coffee shop is open daily until 1 a.m. serving an excellent lunch for 50 cents and an unexcelled dinner for 75 cents Club Breakfast, 35 cents 45 cents and 50 cents. Free Radios in rooms. Rates as low as $2.50 to $3.00 with bath; $1.50 to $2.00 without bath. Ceiling fan in every room. Magnificent fourteen-story annex recently completed. The rooms are large and airy, having both tubs and shower baths and are also provided with running ice water for the convenience of our guests."[34]

Frank Monteleone married Mae Elodie Attaway on June 9, 1927, and the happy couple welcomed a baby boy named William into the world in 1928. James D. Kenney passed away in the summer of 1936. The hotel's management became the responsibility of both Frank Monteleone and Tony Spatafora. Spatafora actually lived in the hotel for a portion of his life, occupying a suite on the fourteenth floor.[35]

Vintage postcard showing the corner of the mezzanine in the hotel.

Opposite page:
An early view from Royal Street, facing toward Canal Street.

Opposite and above: Two 1930s views of the Hotel Monteleone looking down Royal Street.

F. J. MONTELEONE, MNG. DIR.
A. F. SPATAFORA, GEN. MGR.

NEW ORLEANS

The Hotel Monteleone underwent a fourth addition by architects Wogan and Bernard finished in 1956, and the construction created the section that runs down Iberville from Exchange Alley to Royal Street. On to the already massive structure, they added two hundred new rooms, a dining room and cocktail lounges.[36]

New Orleans as a city has always had a fascinating association with the art and artifice of sin. Indiscretion, whether it be gambling, prostitution or imbibing during the period of Prohibition, is as woven into her fabric as the river and the rising heat. The most legendary area of sin in America at one time was New Orleans' own Storyville. Modeled after the red light districts in Europe, Storyville was created in 1898 to house the houses of ill repute and to contain and legalize a black-market area of industry. Curious visitors could find "blue books," which were catalogs describing each brothel's location, services, specialties and pricing lists. Pricing ranged from 50¢ to $10, and the most expensive and lavish ladies were found in the beautiful, rambling mansions on Basin Street. It was thought that by corralling the sale of sex, debaucherous drinking establishments, gambling saloons and wanton behavior in one area, it would leave the rest of the city cleaner, safer and more approachable to tourism and respectable industry.

Storyville's effect on the Hotel Monteleone is undeniable. The district, in a way, affected every hotel in New Orleans both directly and indirectly. During his days, Antonio Monteleone was able to build and operate a clean, proper hotel with a streetfront entrance free from cat calling and hassling thanks to the deviance that was safely contained north of Rampart. Storyville no longer exists, and its demise created the problems that its existence prevented. In the 1940s and beyond, these issues would plague both Antonio Monteleone's son and grandson as they operated the massive hotel.

Storyville fell as World War I began. The federal government outlawed the sale of sex, despite strong objections from the city government, and sin—as it is apt to do—spread underground. Although it was hidden by darkness, it was never eradicated or even diminished. The brothels were converted to dance halls and cabarets, which were simply fronts for speakeasies and continuing prostitution.

A large marquee sign on Canal Street directed guests to the hotel in the 1950s.

HOTEL MONTELEONE

600 ROOMS
FREE RADIOS IN ROOMS
SOME ROOMS AIR-CONDITIONED

SAMPLE ROOMS
GARAGE IN CONNECTION
LARGE PARKING GROUNDS

— CENTER OF ACTIVITY — — IN A CITY OF CHARM —

F. J. MONTELEONE, MANAGING DIRECTOR
A. F. SPATAFORA, GEN'L MANAGER

NEW ORLEANS 12, U.S.A.
December 14, 1949

Mr. Sydney Kaffie
S. H. Kaffie, Inc.
Natchitoches, La

Dear Sydney:

In reply to your letter of December 12th, we are pleased to confirm the reservation of a double room and bath for your occupancy beginning February 17th, to the 22nd, a period of five days.

Please be advised that all reservations are held until 7 P.M. only, unless otherwise notified.

All cancellations must be in 15 days before February 17th.

Looking forward to having you with us, wishing you a very Merry Christmas and a Happy New Year, we remain

Sincerely,

Tony

A. F. "Tony" Spatafora
General Manager

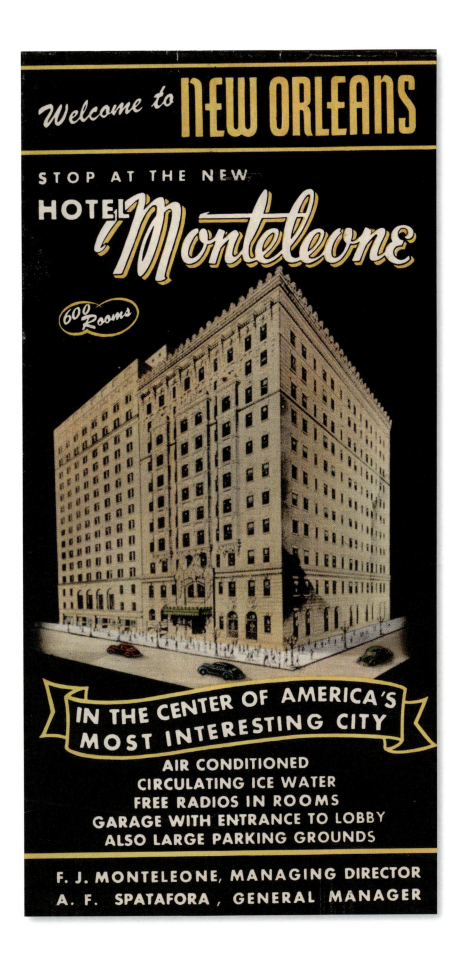

Roof decks were popular additions to many American hotels in the 1950s and '60s. The Monteleone's own construction is shown here in a snapshot from 1963.

William "Billy" Monteleone.

In 1940, Storyville's famous houses were demolished to build the Iberville Project. Sadly, the towering mansions of Basin Street were likewise destroyed in the gutting, and the street for a time was renamed North Saratoga. It was renamed Basin Street eventually and remains that today.

Just as Antonio had fought against men like Otto Schoenhausen, his son and grandson would face the proponents of the world's oldest profession as well as men and women rallying against new zoning developments.

If Antonio Monteleone created the Hotel Monteleone, and Frank and Kenney sustained it, Frank's son William Monteleone would be the man who would hang his hat on modernizing it. The infamous Swan Room, where Liberace was often on the bill, was opened in 1955, and upon Frank's death in 1958, William took over hotel operations, adding six stories to the nine-story portion on Royal and Iberville. The idea of rooftop dining and sunning on sky-high decks by sparkling pools came about for many hotels in the decades of the 1950s and 1960s, and the Hotel Monteleone was no exception. A large swimming pool was added to William's 1963 plans for expansion, which also called for a wading pool, putting green, presidential suite, and nightclub restaurant to be called Sky Lite. The main contractor was F. J. Forstall, and Joseph Grima Bernard was hired as the architect, and the "Sky Terrace" opened in 1964, advertised as "Le Spot Romantique!"[37]

Not everyone in town loved these new advancements. A group of historic preservationists rebuked plans for a new bank and an addition to the hotel in 1963, citing that the building plans would demolish historic properties in the Vieux Carré. Judge Alexander Rainold permitted the razing in a judgment handed down on January 29, 1963.

These years, roughly from the 1940s to the 1970s, were marked by painful growth spurts for the French Quarter. The area once again became a prime location for entrepreneurs looking to capitalize on debauchery. Drinking halls opened rapidly, prostitution found a new home with the destruction of Storyville, and the crime became so rampant that it caught the attention of national news outlets. In response to pressure from historic preservationists, the city banned new drinking halls from being built in designated portions of the French Quarter. A group called the Vieux Carré Commission (VCC), formed in 1936, was under pressure to preserve the city's historic buildings from one side and under pressure to provide demolition permits from the opposition.

Antonio himself had destroyed approximately seven of them in the name of creating the Monteleone property long before the commission was even formed, yet there was a bit of friction between the VCC and the hotel for past transgressions and appeals for more additions.

The docks in these modern decades were filled nightly with sailors on leave and tourists fresh off the boats, all of whom necessitated more entertainment, accommodations and parking. The overwhelming incentive of money-to-be-made eventually toppled the VCC's weak regulations, and in 1946, the protected area of Rampart and one block of Royal were given up to

In the 1960s, the penthouse suites were redone in a contemporary décor for the decade, with large windows offering sweeping views of the city and the Mississippi River.

Advertisement from the 1960s shows an illustration of completed rooftop Sky Lite Lounge.

Overleaf:
Advertisement from the 1960s shows the completed rooftop addition to the hotel.

developers. The constitutional boundaries of these areas were restored in 1964, but it was too late for many beautiful buildings that were razed in the name of progress.[38]

In the '60s, when it was time for Tony Spatafora to retire and step down as manager, William Monteleone surprised a few by his selection of successor. Sam Kennedy was the resident manager during these years, but instead of promoting him to general manager, Monteleone chose a man named Fred Forstall in 1961. Forstall held the position of general manager and executive vice president for two decades, during which he built his own construction company—F.J. Forstall Co., Inc.—and established three real estate companies. Ever busy, ever present in New Orleans life and society—whether it was his involvement working with the Greater New Orleans Tourist and Convention Commission or celebrating Mardi Gras in the krewes of Bacchus, Athenians, Olympia and Mystery—Forstall was a very public figure and a great asset to the hotel.[39]

Forstall's background in construction benefited the hotel as well. He was the man behind the creation of the Queen Anne Ballroom and the construction of the Iberville wing.

Following Forstall in the role of manager was a man named Howard Goodman. Goodman carried on a tradition at the Monteleone that still exists today in management—the tradition of community service far beyond the hotel doors. He served as the president of both the Greater New Orleans Hotel and Motel Association and the Louisiana Hotel Motel Association, and for part of his career, he was the vice president of the Greater New Orleans Tourist & Convention Commission. Sadly, Goodman passed away from cancer less than a decade after accepting the management role at the Hotel Monteleone. Ron Pincus was appointed vice president and chief operating officer in 1990, and with the help of William Monteleone's son William Jr., the hotel realized its current luxury suites. Named for famous writers who were fond of the hotel, guests can today reserve a stay in the Tennessee Williams Suite, the Hemingway Penthouse or the William Faulkner Suite.

The hotel continues to evolve in modern times. In 2001, renovations began yet again, to the tune of $70 million. Unseen conveniences such as new plumbing and air conditioning units

General Manager Howard Goodman.

Vice President and Chief Operating Officer Ron Pincus.

were coupled with openly aesthetic changes like beautiful granite and marble bathroom overhauls and raising the ceilings back to their original heights. A spa was added to the Hotel Monteleone, alongside stunning black-and-white vintage hotel photos lining the hallway from the garage to reception and soundproofing for the rooms. These upgrades were overseen by Ron Pincus. His contributions to the visual aesthetic and modern conveniences along with his ability to keep operations moving seamlessly and simultaneously throughout the construction elevated the hotel mid-project from a three-diamond to a four-diamond property.

Although many of the interior touches remain antiquated for the sake of ambiance, again thanks to Pincus' ingenuity, the events held annually at the Hotel Monteleone bring cutting-edge experts and enthusiasts from around the world. The hotel is headquarters for two massive festivals each year—Words & Music put on by the Pirate's Alley Faulkner Society and the Tales

Overleaf:
The design of the lobby welcomes guests with stunning gilded elegance.

The modern-day rooftop pool at the Hotel Monteleone.

The grandfather clock, now standing in the hotel lobby, was crafted by sculptor Antonio Puccio in 1909. It is made from hand-carved mahogany and has been a part of the Hotel Monteleone's decor for more than a century.

of the Cocktail Festival put on by Ann and Paul Tuennerman. In fact, both events began their very first celebrations at the hotel, and despite growing quite large, they have remained loyal to hosting at the Monteleone.

Tales of the Cocktail welcomes more than ten thousand annually for a five-day extravaganza celebrating the art of the cocktail and the history of the drink. The hotel is completely sold out each year during the event, and opens up meeting rooms, banquet facilities and kitchens to make sure everything runs smoothly, from seminars to the thousands of limes and lemons squeezed for cocktails behind the scenes.

"The Hotel Monteleone embodies the deep, rich, cultural history of the City of New Orleans," says Ann Tuennerman. She's the founder of Tales of the Cocktail, which in the last few years has become the support for her charity, the New Orleans Culinary and Cultural Preservation Society.

"The Monteleone has been our partner from the very beginning, in great years and in trying years, like 2005, immediately following Hurricane Katrina," Ann states.

Hurricane Katrina was definitely trying, to say the least. It affected the city, the state, the nation and the world, and standing against the winds and rising waters, the hotel remained a family and a safe harbor for hundreds in New Orleans.

"We were completely full when Katrina hit," says Andrea Thornton, director of sales and marketing for the property for more than a decade. "We opened up and invited people to stay out the storm inside the hotel. These were people from all over the city who couldn't evacuate for whatever reason. There was no electricity. For previous storms, it was common for people to evacuate to hotels. To party for a few days and then return home. This was a whole different scenario."

With the storm's flooding crippling the city, the hotel closed until October 15, 2005. Members of the management team, like Thornton, called every single employee following the storm to assure them that not only would they be paid, regardless of the hotel being closed, the tipped employees would still receive their average tip wages, and that everyone would be compensated over and above normal salary with hardship wages.

"The hotel really sees the employees as an extended family," Thornton explains. "We hired a psychiatrist to come in and offer free counseling. We had approximately 150 families living here for free for six months after the storm, and we paid regular wages plus meals. Another fifty families were here for an additional three months beyond that."

Every single business lost employees following the storm, many deciding life in the severely damaged city was too hard to return to. The Monteleone was no exception. However, many employees are still slowly trickling back.

"It's such an amazing place to work every day," Thornton muses. "I was working here in the 1970s with my late husband. He worked at the Monteleone for twenty years. I found another job after he passed, but I returned ten years ago. We lost a great deal of employees from Katrina, but we see more and more returning all the time. It has that sense of magic, this hotel."

The hotel in 2010 is scheduled for additional renovations. The Carousel Bar is going to get a bit of a facelift by knocking down the wall that joins it to the Hunt Room Grill and earning a street entrance by sometime in 2011.[42]

Each summer, the Tales of the Cocktail event brings thousands of beverage enthusiasts to the city–directly to the Hotel Monteleone's Carousel Bar, where several events are held.

Employees

The hotel has dozens of employees who have worked on staff for more than three decades. Tony Spatafora was employed by the Hotel Monteleone for more than sixty years, and Bellman Raoul Vives has been there since the 1960s.

Earl Perkins began working as an elevator attendant for the salary of $39 a week in 1966. He worked steadily for three years, after which the hotel taught him how to drive and gave him the new position of valet. Perkins rose to position of garage manager in the 1980s. The garage housed two gas pumps, and guests could get an oil change as well. Twenty-one men were employed in the garage in those decades, but today the job only takes two men a shift, largely thanks to automatic elevators.

"When the parades passed," Perkins recalls, "we had so much business in that garage." The gas pumps were removed in 1990 and the hole for the oil changes was filled in.[43]

"Working for the hotel is like working for family," says Beverly Purdy. Employed for thirty-four years, Purdy began in reservations and has also filled the role of office manager, before moving to her current job in food and beverage accounting.[44]

"Hotel" Al Barros welcomes everyone. Literally. Now the hotel bell captain, he's been reporting for work at Hotel Monteleone for fifty years. He's seen a great deal of important figures, working in roles like the hotel limousine driver for fifteen years and giving driving tours of the French Quarter. In 1995, he welcomed Miss America Heather Whitestone to the Monteleone.

While today it serves only as a valet garage for guests, the hotel's famous neon sign still stands, from the days when you could even get your oil changed at the Monteleone.

Opposite page:
The Monteleone's elegant façade, created by the architecture firm of Toledano & Wogan, is legendary and stands as a physical piece of art in the heart of the French Quarter.

THE NEW HOTEL MONTELEONE

April 27, 1939

DINNER

Fish or Meat .75¢   w Both $1.00
SERVED w SAUTERNE or CLARET WINE

Dill Pickles, Pearl Onions & Olives

Choice of Appetizer   TRUE FRUIT JUICES
Pineapple, Orange, Grapefruit or Celery Juice.
Pressed Pompano Mourtardine, Gulf Shrimp Remoulade
Cold Crabmeat w 1000 Island Dressing.
Assorted Fruit Cocktail, Stuffed Devilled Egg Virginia,

Soup
Vermicelli & Tomato,
Turtle w Sherry, Oyster a la Rene,
Okra Gumbo Creole, Cold Consomme en Jellee.

Choice of Fish
Gulf Tenderloin Trout Meuniere
Baked Oyster on Shell Kilpatrick
Selected Fried Soft Shell Crab Tartar Sauce

or Choice of Entree
Half Spring Chicken Saute a la Maryland
Broiled Veal T Bone Steak Parsley Butter
Creole Crab Omelette Mushroom & Green Peas

Vegetables
Cauliflower Butter Sauce, Steamed Rice,
Lima Beans Fermiere, Demi Julienne Potatoes

Salad
Sliced Hawaiin Pineapple w Grated Cheese

Dessert
Fresh Strawberry Soufflee,
Lemon, Peach, Cocoanut, Vanilla & Apple Pies,
French Caramel Custard, Boston Cream Pie,
Vanilla or Chocolate Ice Cream, Pineapple Sherbert,
Swiss Phyldephia or Roquefort Cheese & Jelly
Milk Iced or Hot Tea or Beer

CHAPTER 3
Food and Entertainment

When one thinks of New Orleans, scent and sound are often initial sensory images. The city is built on zydeco and jazz almost as equally as it is built on oyster po'boys and crawfish etouffee. But rather than fading away to make room for other visions, sight and sound, where New Orleans is concerned, only grow more pungent on the mind.

The Hotel Monteleone has always cultivated and continues to elevate both music and food—ever since Antonio Monteleone first set out his vision in the late 1800s.

Before he acquired the property and changed the name to the Hotel Monteleone, the hotel was the Hotel Victor. Proprietor Victor Bero had a French restaurant in the space that the restaurant Galatoire's now occupies, so he never included dining options in the hotel. In the nineteenth century, women generally dined in the home, but hotels were an exception to this rule. A few high-end lodgings with lavish cuisine during these years included the Tremoulet, St. Charles, and St. Louis.[45]

When the Hotel Monteleone debuted under that appellation in 1909, guests strolled in off the street to an expansive lobby, replete

Opposite page:
A spring menu from 1939 lists delicacies like Pompano and Cold Crabmeat.

Photograph of the lobby entrance to the coffee shop in the 1940s.

In keeping with the overall theme for the bar, little touches, such as the swizzle stick shown here, incorporated artist Enrique Alferez's carving of Leda with the Swan.

Opposite page:
In this 1940s photo, a marquee-styled sign tempts guests with the hotel's new dancing and drinking options.

with a coffee shop and a restaurant. The Monteleone has always held the idea of service in high regard. Food and drink was certainly paramount then and so remains today.

The city of New Orleans has enjoyed a love affair with imbibing strong spirits for centuries. The notorious smuggler and pirate Jean Lafitte is reputed to have operated a bar in the French Quarter as far back as 1772, and even the federal government's passage of Prohibition proved pointless in the modern decades of the '20s and '30s—its iron grip lax where New Orleans was concerned.

The Hotel Monteleone used the restaurant space as a lounge at night after 1933, but there is not much in the way of documented evidence prior to manager A. F. "Tony" Spatafora's decision to open a specific space for drinking, entertainment and dancing. From a 1938 newspaper clipping, we get a great description of the first Swan Room.

"The lounge generally follows the embossed leather and aluminum band motif of the existing cocktail bar and the lighting is not different. But in ceiling and floor, the lounge becomes distinctly individual with mirrors adding to the feeling of space and roominess."[46]

Famous New Orleans sculptor Enrique Alferez was hired to create a piece for the room, which became the focal point. He carved a statue of *Leda with the Swan*, inspired by Antonio Allegri's famous painting of the same name from 1531. The finished statue was placed behind the stage, creating an iconic and stunning backdrop for the musicians who would help make the room famous in decades to come. Other design features in the Swan Room in the late '30s included a circular dance space with an eight-pointed star design in the floor.

Another feature that set the Hotel Monteleone's entertainment options apart was the consideration of the fairer sex. During the 1930s, ladies could enter not only through the lobby lounge entrance, but also through a women-only Royal Street entrance, which led to a private salon and sitting area.

The Second World War helped pull America out of the Great Depression, and the Big Band Era swept through the nation. The Swan Room was host to full-sized bands in the early 1940s, enticing guests with the dances du jour like the rumba, the tango,

At reopening of the Swan room in the Monteleone hotel, New Orleans. Seated, left to right: Mrs. John Ireland (Joanne Dru); Frank J. Monteleone, president and managing director, Monteleone hotel, New Orleans; Mrs. Frank J. Monteleone. Standing: A. F. "Tony" Spatafora, manager, Monteleone hotel, and Robert Mitchum.

On September 23, 1953, the Swan Room reopens with famous faces like Jane Russell, Joanne Dru and Robert Mitchum in attendance.

the Lindy-Hop and the popular swing styles. These days would not last long, however. The "Cabaret Tax" passed in 1944 brought a crashing halt to the Big Band Era. Levied at 20 to 30 percent, this tax was placed on any establishment with a dance floor and alcohol service, forcing bar owners to cut back on hiring expensive orchestra-styled bands.

In 1949, when money was a bit easier, Frank Monteleone, his wife and their son William invited friends and family for a grand re-opening of the sainted Swan Room. The event debuted a new decor courtesy of designer Glenn Flanders of St. Louis, Missouri, and set new hours for the lounge as well. The Swan Room was open every fall, but remained closed each spring in order to turn a profit.[47]

By January of 1950, the Hotel Monteleone's Swan Room was becoming quite the star attraction for visitors to New Orleans. The room's design featured additional sculptures, including a carved white swan with extended wings and a female nude, and light blue and soft grey palette tones throughout. Dinner was served inside from 6 to 9 p.m., followed by dancing and drinking from 10 p.m. to 2 a.m. When it reopened as scheduled in the fall of 1952, film stars Robert Michum and Joanne Dru were captured in a photograph alongside their hosts, Tony Spatafora and Frank Monteleone.

Opposite page top:
Famous New Orleans sculptor Enrique Alferez was hired to create a piece for the Swan Room, which became the focal point. In the photo, his carving of *Leda with the Swan*, is visible behind the stage. Other design features in The Swan Room in the late '30s included a circular dance space with an eight-pointed star design in the floor.

Opposite page bottom:
The bar inside the Swan Room.

Nineteen forty-nine was a landmark year for the hotel in terms of entertaining. In the same season that movie stars were arriving to revel and swing in the Swan Room, the Monteleone announced the grand opening of the city's first and only rotating bar, The Carousel. The venue occupied what was formerly the women's private parlor from the 1930s.

The Carousel originally appeared and operated much as it does today. A single motor still turns the two thousand rollers beneath the floor, moving the barstools on a track around a central, stationary bar. Thus, the patrons rotate around the bartenders while they mix, each full rotation equaling approximately fifteen minutes. An adjoining space provided additional, non-rotating seating and eventually a piano for entertaining.[48]

Shown here, the original Carousel Bar, opened in 1949, took over the space that was previously a ladies-only parlor.

The Carousel Bar has known several designs throughout the decades. Shown here, the big top tent was a grand feature.

The original design of the Carousel Bar was ultimately more circus-esque, with a nod toward art deco in the design. In 1992, the room was updated and carvings were built into the bar design. Eight jester faces were carved into the overhanging outer rim, and eight cherubs smile out from the inner post. Like the Swan Room, the Carousel has always held appeal for celebrities. Greg Allman reportedly claimed a barstool and a spot at the piano one night, and Etta James has also graced the room. John Autin plays regularly now.[49]

Created by bartender Walter Bergeron in 1938, the Vieux Carré cocktail is still an oft-consumed classic at the Carousel Bar.

Vieux Carré Cocktail
Ice Cubes
1/8 tsp. Benedictine
2 dashes Peychaud's Bitters®
2 dashes Angostura Bitters®
3/4 oz. each of rye whiskey, Cognac, Italian vermouth

Combine all ingredients in a rocks glass over ice. Stir and garnish with a lemon twist.

Above:
This illustration shows the canopy in the Carousel Bar.

Right:
The Carousel saw several redesigns before its present incarnation. This photo, taken sometime in the 1960s, shows the view from the piano lounge looking toward the revolving bar.

A. F. "TONY" SPATAFORA
General manager of the Monteleone hotel, New Orleans, greets Lee Liberace, renowned piano artist, on his arrival at the Monteleone, where he was the guest of Frank and Isabel Monteleone and Tony Spatafora. Immediately following his engagement in New Orleans at the Municipal Auditorium he spent the week-end at Pass Christian, Miss., at "Montebella"—the home of Isabel and Frank Monteleone.

Louis Prima was extremely fond of the city of New Orleans. He played frequent shows at the Sky Lite Lounge in the mid-1960s, and in this photo you can see the Monteleone crest that is still on the wall just outside the elevator doors at the rooftop pool.

These were the glory days of the beloved lobby bar at the Monteleone. Looking back, a few of the performers now seem a bit humorous, given that they occasionally displayed circus-esque talents. Acts ran for two weeks at a time, and the Swan Room hosted Myrus, the mentalist, and also Tung-Pin-Soo, billed as a magician from the Orient.

Musicians especially coveted the room, and Spatafora managed to reel guests in with advertisements announcing names like Dorothy Lamar, Nelson Eddy, Tito Guzar, Nick Lucas, Jane Russell, Marie McDonald, and Leo Carrello.

In March of 1958, actress and singer Corinne Calvet performed in the Swan Room, giving her renditions of "Running Wild," "Autumn Leaves" and "You'd Be So Nice to Come Home To."[50]

Perhaps the most famous two men to ever create music and merriment inside of the Monteleone—whether it was on the rooftop or down in the Swan Room—were Liberace and Louis Prima. Both men were common fixtures at the hotel, never remaining for too long, but never failing to return either.

Louis Prima was just twenty-two years of age when he opened The Famous Door club in New York City. The year was 1935, and the New Orleans-born trumpet player wowed audiences eager for swing music. In fact, he was one of the few performers to survive and thrive during the trying years under the Cabaret Tax. Although he operated out of New York, New Orleans held a special place for Prima, and specifically friendship with the Monteleone family. In 1964, the hotel announced the re-opening after the brand new addition, including the redone rooftop terrace and the Sky Lite Lounge.

Prima's own family still resided in New Orleans, and by the early 1970s, he was set to contract regular performances at the Economy Hall venue inside the Royal Sonesta Hotel in the Quarter. The deal went south, and the Monteleone family jumped at the opportunity, offering Prima a regular gig at Sky Lite. Sadly, he would only play there for just under one year, passing away in 1978.[51]

By the time Liberace opened at the Las Vegas Rivera Hotel as the highest paid entertainer in Vegas history, he had performed at the Hotel Monteleone several times. His charisma and piano skills made him a natural fit for the rebel-rousing wild and free city of New Orleans. At one point in the 1950s, he spent a month

From left to right: Tony Spatafora, Frank Monteleone and Liberace.

of his tour at the Monteleone, and in 1953, he stayed on as a guest during his sold-out show at the Municipal Auditorium.[52] The days of the Swan Room and Sky Lite were numbered. The hotel management went through a series of hurdles with redesigning and renaming the Swan Room during the second half of the 1900s. The name and concept were changed multiple times, from Le Chasseur to the Supper Club and even Steaks Unlimited. One reincarnation as "The Men's Grill" caused an uproar among feminist groups and a lawsuit in 1973. It was overturned by the U.S. Circuit Court of Appeal, but the hotel management changed the name anyway.[53] The Hunt Room was announced shortly after, and instead of dancing, dining became the focus, with grilled prime sirloin steak prepared tableside followed by bananas foster set to fire.[54] It remains today, sharing part of the first level with the elegant but comfortable Le Café.[55] Le Café serves breakfast and lunch, closing at 2 p.m. so that the staff can set up the Hunt Club for supper every evening.

In the 1980s, William Monteleone, known affectionately as "Billy," instituted the Aft Deck Oyster Bar, which earned acclaim in the *New York Times* for the oyster soup, but ultimately closed its doors before too long to make space for the Royal Meeting rooms.

The Queen Anne Ballroom has played host to a plethora of events over the years. Frank Monteleone named the room after his

William Monteleone's contribution of the Aft Deck Oyster Bar garnered praise from the *New York Times* for the oysters. A highlight during the 1980s, today the space is occupied by the Royal Meeting rooms.

granddaughter Anne. In 1965, Anne's room would promote both jazz and swing music with an eight-week event called "Swingin' at the Monteleone." Admission was $1.50, and for eight Saturdays that year, guests were treated to the musical styling of artists like Papa Celestin's Original Tuxedo Band, Armand Hug Trio, The Last Straws and Sweet Emma. Bandleader Pinky Vidacovich stood in as master of ceremonies.[56] According to an unidentified newspaper clipping from October 28, 1963, Vidacovich spotted local talent in the audience one evening and all but begged Helen Keeting Schuler to sing a few songs with the band. She finally agreed, and according to the article, "stole the show from a lineup of all star jazz talent."

The previously professional singer performed "Some of These Days" and "Lazy River" before returning to her seat in the audience.[57] Today the Carousel Bar remains open nearly twenty-four hours, and just as they did decades ago, the bartenders must jump over the bartop to get out when they need something. There is no door on the revolving circle.

Marvin Allen has been working there for decades, honing a fine skill in mixology and crafted cocktails thanks to his forerunners like Walter Bergeron and new events like Tales of the Cocktail. Bergeron is credited with creating the Vieux Carré Cocktail in 1938. Still consumed today around the world, the drink takes its name from the French term meaning, "Old Quarter."

Tales of the Cocktail welcomes tens of thousands of cocktail enthusiasts annually to the city of New Orleans, and more specifically the Hotel Monteleone, where it anchors. The week-long event offers competitions, seminars, tastings, parties and book signings, all focused on bringing the art of bartending back to what it once was before Prohibition.

The Nine-to-Five bar was a rooftop meeting spot at the hotel in the 1960s. Guests enjoyed cold cocktails and a stunning view of the Mississippi River moving below.

Opposite page:
The current Carousel Bar design includes eight carved jester faces on the outer rim of the canopy.

CHAPTER 4
Prose, Plots, and Bon Vivants

Things *happen* in hotels. Business deals are sealed with a firm handshake in lavish lobby restaurants, and elevators doors open on unsuspecting couples kissing. Loud bumps in the night lead guests to discuss ghosts over cups of coffee in the morning, and grand ballrooms are elegant backdrops to weddings and anniversary parties. There's music, and there's art. There's pizzazz and panache. There's history made more elaborate by the guests that grace a hotel's halls, especially those that are famous.

The Hotel Monteleone has seen authors, actresses, musicians, athletes, dignitaries, dowagers and debutants aplenty. They come to visit, and they leave with a desire to weave their experience in this old hotel into songs, books, manuscripts and plays, returning time and time again to soak up a bit of that joie de vivre that the hotel has nourished over the years.

The Pen and the Page

It's not surprising that hotels make wonderful settings for characters in literature. They are convenient houses of happening, and novelists themselves often find inspiration within. You might say that they are apt stage settings for prose, both fictitious and true.

The Hotel Monteleone is one of the most glorified hotels featured in American literature. Designated as a national literary landmark in 1999 by the American Library Association, the hotel is mentioned in the works of many of the major Southern authors of the last century—acclaimed men and women of the pen including Eudora Welty, William Faulkner, Truman Capote and Anne Rice—as well as writers beyond the Mason-Dixon line. The hotel has not only set a stage for many a plot to progress, it also set a very real social scene for the authors themselves.

Author William Faulkner moved to the Crescent City for the first time in 1925 from Oxford, Mississippi. Legend claims that he

William Faulkner moved to New Orleans from Mississippi in 1925 and made his home at 624 Pirate's Alley.

For author Tennessee Williams, the hotel was not only a favorite place to stay in New Orleans, but a favorite scene setting for many of his plays.

Truman Capote was particularly fond of the Monteleone, even going so far as to claim he was born inside the hotel. While untrue, the story became a bit of legend often associated with the author.

arrived to meet fellow writer Sherwood Anderson wearing a coat lined with hidden bottles of booze, for fear that he might not find alcohol in the city.[58] New Orleans stole a piece of his heart in the '20s, and Faulkner's adoration for the city and the hotel remained alive and well for decades in both his works—which frequently mention the Hotel Monteleone—and in his repeated trips to stay at the hotel. He spent a portion of his honeymoon with his wife Estelle Oldham at the Hotel Monteleone in 1929, in the same year he was penning what is considered by some his most illustrious work, *The Sound and the Fury*.[59] He checked in again in 1951, with his wife, mother and several family members, to conduct an interview with Albert Goldstein about his receiving a Legion d'Honneur, France's esteemed award for extraordinary achievements. Goldstein was a co-founder of the 1920s literary journal *The Double Dealer*, which was the first paper to publish any of Faulkner's works. Much later, Faulkner's biographer Joseph Blotner would site the Hotel Monteleone as the author's favorite hotel in the world. Today, his works and his love of the Monteleone are promoted and championed by the current New Orleans–based Pirate's Alley Faulkner Society and their annual Words & Music event, which is headquartered at Hotel Monteleone.

The 1950s also played host to another writer who called himself Tennessee Williams. Born Thomas Lanier Williams, "Tennessee" checked in with his grandfather, Rev. Walter Dakin, and at the end of a two-week stay, Frank Monteleone picked up their check as a "thank you" to a man who brought pride and national notice to the city with his works. Giving the city immortality and bringing the hotel's name to the common vernacular with his plays like *A Streetcar Named Desire*, Williams spent countless hours in the Hotel Monteleone's Carousel Bar looking for plots and gossip from surrounding tables. His lively characters were formed from days and nights spent in the city and, more specifically, the hotel. In 1948, Williams was awarded a Pulitzer Prize for Drama for *Streetcar*, and in 1952 his work *The Rose Tattoo* received a Tony Award for Best Play. Within *The Rose Tattoo*, he uses the Hotel Monteleone as a symbol of the city's dichotomy of traditional gentility and forward thinking.[60]

Truman Capote was so enamored with the romance and glamour of the Monteleone that he constantly claimed he was

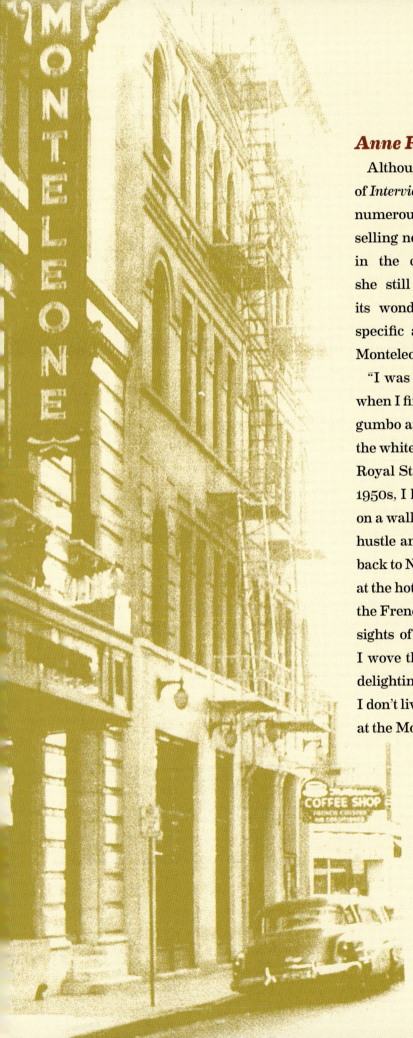

Anne Rice

Although Anne Rice, author of *Interview with the Vampire* and numerous other nationally best selling novels, no longer resides in the city of New Orleans, she still holds a fondness for its wonderful enclaves, and a specific affection for the Hotel Monteleone.

"I was a little girl of eleven, so it must have been 1952, when I first visited the hotel coffee shop and was treated to gumbo and crackers there. I thought it very lovely. Loved the white linen. I loved the lobby and found the location on Royal Street very exciting. When I was a teenager in the 1950s, I loved to walk through the lobby whenever I was on a walking date in the French Quarter. I remember the hustle and bustle, the glamour, and the charm. On visits back to New Orleans from California in the 1970s, I stayed at the hotel, and again loved its location, right at the gate of the French Quarter, and its proximity to all the wonderful sights of the Quarter. After my return to New Orleans, I wove this beautiful hotel into my novels when I could, delighting in writing about it as a New Orleans institution. I don't live in New Orleans now, but I would probably stay at the Monteleone if I went back for a visit."

born inside the hotel. It was an outright yet beloved lie. His mother, sixteen-year-old beauty queen Lillie Mae Faulk, was living in the hotel when she was pregnant. However, Capote was actually born in the Touro Infirmary.[61]

Female authors were and are no strangers to the hotel. Short story writer Eudora Welty's hometown of Jackson, Mississippi, lies just hours north of New Orleans, and in 1935 she stayed at the hotel with a girlfriend named Migs Schermerhorn. In a biography of Welty by Suzanne Marrs, Marrs recounts the wild events of their stay. A few men attempted to play a prank on the women, labeling the men's bathroom as the women's and vice versa. Welty was not to be intimidated, and she complained to the hotel staff and had a hotel employee stationed outside the hallway bathrooms to make sure nothing of the sort happened again.[62]

Eudora Welty, pictured here, was a guest in 1935.

Modern-day writer Anne Rice has mentioned the Hotel Monteleone several times in her dark, driven works like *The Witching Hour* and *Memnoch the Devil*, and the lighter yet haunted *Hallowed Bones* by Carolyn Haines also places characters in the hotel periodically. In *Divine Secrets of the Ya-Ya Sisterhood* and *Ya-Yas in Bloom*, author Rebecca Wells settles her characters into the Monteleone for a night or two as well.

Today the hotel's largest and most elaborate suites are named for several of the noteworthy literary names that have graced the halls in the past. Guests can reserve the Tennessee Williams Suite, the William Faulkner Suite or the Hemingway Penthouse, named for Ernest Hemingway and his tribute to the Monteleone in his short story, "The Night Before Battle."[63]

Thanks to a long love affair with the written word, the hotel has now become the official hotel for a number of literary events. The Tennessee Williams Festival occurs each March, followed by an event called Pen to Press every May. In September, writers descend for Heather Graham's New York Writers Conference, and in November the Pirate's Alley Faulkner Society puts on the Words & Music festival.

A Literary Landmark

When the Hotel Monteleone was designated as a Literary Landmark by the American Library Association in 1999, novelist Richard Ford was the honoree. He spoke passionately about the city and the hotel's impact on his memories of childhood.

"My father took me to the Monteleone for the first time in 1948, and he kept on taking me to the Monteleone until 1960. So my whole early experience of New Orleans emanated from that end of Royal Street. I remember looking out the window of the room and dreaming. And there's another wonderful memory of my father and mother and me in the Carousel Bar. My father and my mother were having a drink, and I was sitting on the bar. Suddenly my father got a look of profound consternation on his face, and he said, 'God, I might have gotten drunk here.'

And my mother said, 'What do you mean?'

[He replied,] 'I mean that one drink's gone to my head. When I came in this bar I thought we were on the other side of the room.' He had no idea, sweet man that he was, that that bar was just slowly inching around."

Ford set a portion of his first work, *A Piece of My Heart*, at the Hotel Monteleone.

The authors who have sipped cocktails in the Carousel Bar, enjoyed the sun on the roof terrace and put their heads against soft pillows to sleep are plentiful. Many have gone on to immortalize the Monteleone name in print. A few include:

- *A Farewell to Justice* by Joan Mellen
- *Almost Innocent* by Sheila Bosworth
- *The Complete Short Stories of Ernest Hemingway* by John, Patrick and Gregory Hemingway
- *Mosquitoes* by William Faulkner and Frederick R. Karl
- *Huey Long Invades New Orleans: The Siege of a City, 1934-36* by Garry Boulard
- *Little Altars Everywhere* by Rebecca Wells
- *Rearview Mirror Looking Back at the FBI, the CIA and Other Tails* by William Turner
- *Black Sunday* by Thomas Harris
- *Crazy in Alabama* by Mark Childress
- *The American Homefront* by Alistair Cook
- *The Boy Who Followed Ripley* by Patricia Highsmith
- *Black Like Me* by John Howard

Vice President and Chief Operating Officer Ron Pincus with Richard Ford, photographed in 1999.

Setting the Stage

Actors and actresses frequent the hotel when staying in the Big Easy for work or pleasure. A long list of movies have been filmed in the hotel, as well, including:

Double Jeopardy
Shot: 1999
Starring: Ashley Judd and Tommy Lee Jones
On Location in: the lobby, front of the hotel and the Carousel Piano Bar and Lounge.

Glory Road
Shot: September 2004
Starring: Josh Lucas, Derek Luke and Jon Voight
On Location in: the lobby

The Last Time
Shot: September 2005
Starring: Brendan Fraser and Michael Keaton
On Location in: the Lobby, Carousel Bar, Hunt Room Grill, Bagatelle and Engineer

Retirement
Shot: February 2005
Starring: Peter Faulk
On Location in: the hotel's Hunt Room Grill

In March of 2008, A&E filmed an episode of *Criss Angel Mindfreak* in the Eudora Welty Suite, the lobby, and on the rooftop by the Marquis. Criss Angel is shown here with the hotel's Vice President and Chief Operating Officer, Ron Pincus.

12 Rounds
Shot: March 2008
Starring: John Cena
On Location in: the Vieux Carré Suite (1480), 14th floor hallway, roof by the Marquis, boiler room, garage freight elevator, lobby and front of hotel

The hotel has made its debut visually on the small screen numerous times. A few of the television shows that have filmed at the Monteleone are:

The Travel Channel—"Get Packing"
Shot: November 2003
The Recap: The Hotel Monteleone was the destination backdrop for the winners of a dating game show.

**Food Network—
"Food Nation with Bobby Flay"**
Shot: December 2003
The Recap: Legendary spice-loving chef Bobby Flay hosted a show on the most unique bars in the Big Easy, and the Monteleone's Carousel Bar was among several featured.

**HDTV Production Company—
"Ghoulish Gala 2004"**
Shot: October 2004
The Recap: HDTV Production Company visited the hotel and filmed part of a show centered around the celebration of Halloween in New Orleans.

CBS—"Morning Show"
Shot: March 2005
The Recap: You can catch the Hotel Monteleone's doorman in action on this episode with the line, "Welcome to the Hotel Monteleone. I always start my day with the CBS Morning Show."

NBC—"Today Show"
Shot: October 2007
The Recap: This episode of the Today Show featured a discussion of one of the building's resident ghosts, a young boy named Maurice.

Ghosts

New Orleans is a "spirited" city in many ways. The past is woven into the present in this place, and the spirits of the dead are often discussed as remaining among the living. The Hotel Monteleone is no exception. In fact, it's a pretty exceptional place where spirits and ghosts are concerned.

Andrea Thornton is the director of sales and marketing for the hotel. In her decade of service, she's seen the work of spirits first hand.

"I was in the lobby one day talking to our public relations representative, Bonnie Warren," Thornton recalls. "We both saw the doors to Le Café open and close. We lock those doors every day at 2 p.m., and this was well past that time. We've also had a few guests tell us about ghosts of children playing in some of the rooms on the fourteenth floor."[64]

In 2003 Dr. Larry Montz, a renowned field parapsychologist and founder of the International Society of Paranormal Research, visited the hotel for a documentary on spirits. One of a few accredited parapsychologists in the world, Montz employs a combination of science, equipment such as thermal cameras, and his hand-picked team of clairvoyants to help contact entities in haunted places. The hotel was a hot bed of activity.

"We caught the doors of Le Café opening on camera," Montz explains. "We shut the doors, locked them once more, and they opened again."

The explanation? Through research, it was unearthed that that portion of the hotel was once a maintenance room where an engineer named "Red" had spent decades working. Despite still locking the doors every day at 2 p.m., the staff accepts that Red may occasionally have his way and reopen them.

"We actually picked up fourteen entities on site," Montz explains, "from small boys to adults."

He offers that while the Hotel Monteleone is special in many ways, haunting is as common in hotels as hand soap and bellhops.

"Most hotels are haunted," he continues. "People remain there because they loved the hotel, or they decide that they want to reside in a property because it's constantly active with the living. I've been doing this for thirty-eight years," he muses. "When you talk about thirteen blocks in the French quarter, there is so much activity. I would venture it's certainly one of the most haunted places in the world, but not in a scary, evil way portrayed by television and movies. In the real world, 90 percent of these entities that remain are not malevolent. They stay because they loved the place and it's a happy environment."[65]

Endnotes

1. Richard Gambino, *Vendetta: A True Story of the Worst Lynching in America, the Mass Murder of Italian-Americans in New Orleans in 1891, the Vicious Motivations Behind It, and the Tragic Repercussions That Linger to this Day* (Garden City: Doubleday & Company, Inc., 1977), p. 49

2. New Orleans Tourism and Marketing Corporation, *A Slice of Sicily*, http://www.neworleansonline.com/neworleans/multicultural/multiculturalhistory/italian.html

3. Federal Bureau of Investigations, *Italian Organized Crime Overview*, http://www.fbi.gov/hq/cid/orgcrime/lcnindex.htm

4. New Orleans Tourism and Marketing Corporation, *A Slice of Sicily*, http://www.neworleansonline.com/neworleans/multicultural/multiculturalhistory/italian.html

5. *Daily Picayune*. August 6, 1913, p. 3

6. Act before W. O. Hart, July 26, 1882, COB 116, p. 446.

7. Act before Octave Morel, February 20, 1886, COB 124, p. 66. It is an unfortunate fact of history that the next Conveyance Office book, No. 125, is missing, the only such book in the office.

8. Act before Abel Dreyfous, April 14, 1883, COB 118, p. 158.

9. Jules F. Meunier, N.P., June 10, 1886; James Fahey, N.P., May 10, 1893.

10. Samuel Flower, N.P., May 25, 1894. From a fact sheet prepared in the 1980s. Antonio embedded a mosaic of his family crest in the sidewalk at the entrance to his shoe store located at 241 Royal Street, now Rothschild Antiques. The Monteleone crest was used as the imprint in his handmade shoes.

11. *Daily Picayune*, April 22, 1890, p. 5.

12. Sanborn Insurance map for 1885.

13. Clipping from *The Mascot*, September 18, 1886, p. 1.

14. *Daily States*, October 29, 1891, p. 4.

15. Jas. A. Koehl et als vs. Otto H. Schoenhausen, Docket No. 11,658, Louisiana Supreme Court archives, UNO.

16. Koehl vs Schoenhausen, Defense Brief, p. 3-4.

17. Koehl vs Schoenhausen, p. 82.

18. *Daily Picayune*, January 4, 1898, p. 5.

19. Unidentified clipping regarding the purchase on May 19, 1902, before C. T. Soniat of the Duncan Buildings.

20. Hotel Monteleone Clippings archives, 1910, no citation.

21. John S. Kendall, *History of New Orleans* (1922: Lewis Publishing Company, Chicago), v. II, p. 692.

22. *Architectural Art and Its Allies*, vol. 6 (1911), p. 19.

23. *Daily Picayune*, April 8, 1908, p. 5 and November 27, 1908, p. 16; *Architectural Art and Its Allies*, III (January 1908), p. 7.

24. *Daily Picayune*, March 9, 1910, p. 5; September 26, 1910, p. 6.

25. *Daily Picayune*, May 6, 1906, p. 23.

26. *Daily Picayune*, June 16, 1901, p. 3.

27. *Daily Picayune*, October 26, 1910, p. 10.

28. *Daily Picayune*. August 6, 1913, p. 3.

29. Succession Anthony Monteleone, Civil District Court #105,427, cab. 5, roll 8386. Judgment signed July 1921.

30. *Daily Picayune*, August 9, 1913,. p. 1. Monteleone suffered from asthma.

31. Sally K. Evans Reeves and William D. Reeves, *Historic City Park: New Orleans* (New Orleans: City Park Improvement Association, 2000), p. 152.

32. Clipping 1926, Hotel Monteleone Archives.

33. Sale before A. J. Cuneo, July 19, 1916, COB 285/269; Sale before A. B. Leopold, May 29, 1918 COB 297/461; Sale before A. B. Leopold, February 17, 1926, COB 412/51, New Orleans Notarial Archives.

34. Unidentified clipping, 1931, in Hotel Monteleone Archives.

35. Interview with Marlene Bogatche, February 17, 2010, formerly Executive Secretary of the hotel.

36. *Daily States*, January 22, 1955, p.. 26 c. 5. Announced plans for the nine-story replacement of the Commercial Hotel.

37. *Times Picayune*, November 13, 1964.

38. Hilary Irvin, Vieux Carré Commission History. City of New Orleans.

39. *Times Picayune*, June 25, 2003.

40. Interview with Marlene Bogatche, February 17, 2010.

41. Interview with Andrea Thornton. May 29, 2010.

42. Interview with Andrea Thornton. May 29, 2010.

43. Interview Earl Perkins. September 17, 2009.

44. Interview with Beverly Purdy, September 15, 2009.

45. Susan Tucker, ed., *New Orleans Cuisine: Fourteen Signature Dishes and Their Histories* (Jackson, MS: University Press of Mississippi, 2009), p. 14.

46. Newspaper clipping dated August 27, 1938, but with no attribution. Hotel Monteleone archives.

47. *New Orleans States*. January 15, 1950.

48. *Times-Picayune*, August 29, 1999. Clipping Hotel Monteleone Archives.

49. Jennifer Adams, *Phillip Collier's Mixing New Orleans, Cocktails & Legends* (New Orleans: Philbeau Publishing, 2007), p. 65.

50. *Times-Picayune*, July 15, 2001.

51. *States-Item*, August 31, 1974.

52. *Times Picayune*, August 28, 1953; November 17,1965.

53. *Millenson vs. New Hotel Monteleone*, 475 F. 2 d 736, filed May 18, 1972.

54. *Cuisine, The Insider's guide to Local Dining*, March 2, 1999, Hotel Monteleone Archives.

55. *New York Times*, December 28, 1983.

56. Unattributed clipping, November 21, 1963, Hotel Monteleone Archives.

57. Unattributed clipping, October 28, 1963, Hotel Monteleone Archives.

58. Jennifer Adams, *Phillip Collier's Mixing New Orleans, Cocktails & Legends* (New Orleans: Philbeau Publishing, 2007), p. 93.

59. Joel Williamson, *William Faulkner and Southern History* (New York: Oxford University Press, 1993), p. 223.

60. Tennessee Williams, *Plays 1937-1955* (New York: Library of America, 2000), p. 677.

61. Jennifer Adams, *Phillip Collier's Mixing New Orleans, Cocktails & Legends* (New Orleans: Philbeau Publishing, 2007), p. 69.

62. Suzanne Marrs, *Eudora Welty: a biography* (Orlando, Fl: Harcourt, 2005), p. 49.

63. Michael S. Reynolds, *Hemingway: the 1930s* (New York: W. W. Norton Company, 1997), p. 234

64. Interview with Andrea Thornton. May 29, 2010.

65. Interview with Phyllis Paulsen, "There's a Ghost in My Room."

The original bar in the lobby in the early 1900s.

Photo Credits

Page 2: Hotel postcard, hotel archives

Pages 4 and 5: Rooftop photograph by John T. Mendes, the Historic New Orleans Collection, accession no. 2003.0182.74

Page 6: Hotel exterior, photograph by Michael Terranova

Page 10: Antonio Monteleone photograph, hotel archives

Page 13: French Quarter photograph, Bergeron Gallery

Page 15: Mosaic photograph by Scott Carroll

Page 16: Hotel Victor photograph, the Historic New Orleans Collection, accession no. 75-327-RL

Page 19: Postcard, hotel archives

Page 20: Exchange Alley photograph, the Historic New Orleans Collection, accession no. VCS Sq. 36

Page 22: French Quarter map, the Library of Congress

Page 24: Architectural drawing, the Historic New Orleans Collection, accession no. VCS Sq. 35

Page 25: Postcard, hotel archives

Page 27: Antonio Monteleone portrait, courtesy of hotel archives

Pages 28 and 29: Monteleone Gate photograph by Charles L. Franck/Franck-Bertacci Photographers Collection, the Historic New Orleans Collection, accession no. 1979.325.5791

Page 30: Advertisement, hotel archives

Pages 32 and 33: Postcard, hotel archives

Page 34: Frank Monteleone and hotel archives postcard, hotel archives

Page 35: Royal Street, the Historic New Orleans Collection, accession no. VCS Sq. 35

Page 36: Royal Street, the Historic New Orleans Collection, accession no. 1979.325.4550

Page 37: Postcard, hotel archives

Page 38: Advertisement, hotel archives

Page 39: Canal Street, the Historic New Orleans Collection, accession no. 1979.325.4953

Page 40: Letter and bill, hotel archives

Page 41: Brochure cover, hotel archives

Page 42: William Monteleone, photograph by C. Bennette Moore; Roof deck construction photograph by Charles L. Franck/Franck-Bertacci Photographers Collection, the Historic New Orleans Collection, accession no. 1994.942.956

Page 43: Penthouse photo, hotel archives; SkyLite Lounge illustration, hotel archives

Pages 44 and 45: Rooftop illustration, hotel archives

Page 46: Howard Goodman, hotel archives; Ron Pincus photograph by Donn Young; Pool photograph by Michael Terranova

Pages 48 and 49: Lobby photograph by Ron Calamia

Page 50: Clock photograph, hotel archives

Page 51: Carousel Bar photograph by courtesy of Tales of the Cocktail

Page 52: Hotel front photograph by Scott Carroll

Page 53: Garage sign photograph by Scott Carroll

Page 54: Menu and postcard, hotel archives

Page 55: Coffee shop photograph, the Historic New Orleans Collection, accession no. 1979.325.4553

Page 56: Swan Room illustration and swizzle stick, hotel archives

Page 57: Royal Street photograph, New Orleans Public Service

Pages 58 and 59: Swan Room diners photograph, and Liberace photograph, hotel archives

Page 60: Top photograph, hotel archives; Bottom bar photograph, the Historic New Orleans Collection, accession no. 1979.325.4557

Page 61: Advertisement card, hotel archives

Page 62: Postcard, hotel archives

Page 63: Carousel Bar postcard, hotel archives; drink photograph by Michael Terranova

Pages 64 and 65: Carousel Bar illustration and postcard, hotel archives

Page 66: *Hotel World-Review* clipping, hotel archives; Photograph courtesy of Gia Maione Prima/The Louis Prima Estate Archives

Page 67: Liberace photograph by Nancye Photo Studio; Aft Desk Oyster Bar photograph, hotel archives

Page 68: Nine-to-Five Bar photograph, hotel archives

Page 69: Carousel Bar photograph by Charles Chenier

Page 70: Photograph of writing ephemera by Michael Terranova

Page 71: Photograph of William Faulkner by Carl Van Vechten, 1948, Library of Congress, Prints and Photographs Division, Carl Van Vechten Collection (reproduction number, e.g. LC-DIG-ppmsca-10445)

Page 72: Photograph of Tennessee Williams, Billy Rose Theatre Division, The New York Public Library for the Performing Arts, Astor, Lenox and Tilden Foundation. Truman Capote by Carl Van Vechten, 1948, Library of Congress, Prints and Photographs Division, Carl Van Vechten Collection (reproduction number, e.g. LC-USZ62-54231)

Page 73: Photograph of Anne Rice courtesy of Anne Rice

Page 74: Photograph of Eudora Welty by Kay Bell, courtesy of Eudora Welty LLC

Page 75: Photograph of Ron Pincus and Richard Ford, hotel archives

Page 76: Photograph of Criss Angel, hotel archives

Page 77: Rooftop photograph by Lori Cernak

Page 79: Bar photograph, the Historic New Orleans Collection, accession no. 1979.325.4557